FUCK *This* SHITSHOW

FUCK *This* SHITSHOW

A Gratitude Journal *for* Tired-Ass Women

....

KRISTIE BREEN

SIMON ELEMENT

New York   London   Toronto   Sydney   New Delhi

SIMON
ELEMENT

An Imprint of Simon & Schuster, Inc.
1230 Avenue of the Americas
New York, NY 10020

This Simon Element trade paperback edition July 2022

SIMON ELEMENT is a trademark of Simon & Schuster, Inc.

For information about special discounts for bulk purchases,
please contact Simon & Schuster Special Sales at 1-866-506-1949
or business@simonandschuster.com.

The Simon & Schuster Speakers Bureau can bring authors to your
live event. For more information or to book an event, contact the
Simon & Schuster Speakers Bureau at 1-866-248-3049 or visit our
website at www.simonspeakers.com.

Interior design by Jennifer Chung

Cocktails and Wine and Cheese by Olga from the Noun Project
Crown and Middle Finger by Maria Zamchy from the Noun Project
Labyrinth by Alexander Skowalsky from the Noun Project
Mandalas by Abhiraami Thangavel from the Noun Project
Pineapple by Icons Producer from the Noun Project
Stars by Alex Muravev from the Noun Project
Sun by Jenie Tomboc from the Noun Project
Sunglasses by Ash Jones from the Noun Project

Manufactured in the United States of America

1   3   5   7   9   10   8   6   4   2

Library of Congress Cataloging-in-Publication Data has been applied for.

ISBN 978-1-6680-0609-2
ISBN 978-1-6680-0610-8 (ebook)

for 23, 74, and 3
don't ever let me catch you talking like this

i love you

For those of you who know me, *hello!* For those of you who don't, let me explain. My name is Kristie, and I'm a forty-three-year-old mompreneur of three beautiful children who bring me more happiness (and sometimes headaches) than I ever could have imagined.

But I've got a foul mouth. And I'm from Jersey. I don't take shit lying down, and I don't like fake things. Even though I like to be mindful and focus on happiness, I loathe flowery and run-of-the-mill "gratitude journals." I know how to play the game in corporate America, but a lot of the time, I can't wait to hang up on some calls and just cuss it out in private.

So back in 2018, I went to work on a project. I created a brand, Crazy Tired Beetches, and published a handful of journals that mainly focused on one thing: feeling gratitude through laughter. The journals were filled with opportunities to weigh the good and the bad, rant about shit days, celebrate success, and move on— while hopefully feeling better.

Turns out that a lot of other people felt the same way. I made the Amazon Top 50 Best Sellers list. I sold hundreds of thousands of copies. I heard from numerous women who were undergoing chemotherapy or suffering from chronic disease, and many more who just wanted an honest place to vent. They loved the ability to talk freely about how much things sucked and how much they were still blessed.

Then I heard from my good friends at Simon Element, and we decided to expand the original and get it into the hands of even more readers. Which brings us here.

This journal was designed with the best of intentions. It's for you to sit down with a glass of wine (or not) after a long and maybe shitty day, harness your alter ego, then move on with a clear head and focus on your priorities. It's to share with your girlfriends and laugh about over dinner. It's to keep you focused on the positive, but to also acknowledge that life is messy and sometimes things suck. Most important, it's your safe space. It's a place where you can take a moment and complain without judgment—then put the shit behind you and focus on what you love most.

My hope is that you will find some value in journaling away those shitty days, and then refocus your attention on positive things and find laughter in everyday moments.

–K.B.

P.S.: I hope you'll join me on social media: @tiredasswomen on Facebook and Instagram.

DATE:

___ / ___ / ___

DAY OF THE WEEK

(S) (M) (T) (W) (T) (F) (S)

ASSHOLE *of the* DAY:

....
....
....
....

🍍 **FUCK YEAH!** 🍍

Grateful I did this today:

Happy I didn't do this today:

Oh, for fuck's sake.

This didn't go **MY WAY:**

....
....
....

My Mood Today (in pineapples)

🍍 🍍 🍍 🍍 🍍 🍍 🍍 🍍 🍍 🍍

CURRENT MOOD:

- [ ] Happy
- [ ] Leave me the fuck alone
- [ ] Apathetic
- [ ] Grateful
- [ ] Need a nap
- [ ] Other: _____

Wake up.
Make up.
Fuck up.
Repeat.

My fucking **HERO:**

....
....
....
....
....

I've got an **ATTITUDE** *of* **GRATITUDE:**

DATE:

___ / ___ / ___

S M T W T F S

ASSHOLE *of the* DAY:

BITCH *session:*

COLOR THIS SHIT

Today's **SHIT LIST**
(people, places, things):

- [ ] ....
- [ ] ....
- [ ] ....
- [ ] ....
- [ ] ....

- [ ] ....
- [ ] ....
- [ ] ....
- [ ] ....
- [ ] ....

I'm **LUCKY** *to have . . .*

What the **FUCK** *was this?!*

JOURNAL SOME SHIT
that makes you smile:

....

....

....

....

....

My Mood Today (in pineapples)

🍍 🍍 🍍 🍍 🍍 🍍 🍍 🍍 🍍 🍍

DATE:

__ / __ / __

ASSHOLE *of the* DAY:

....
....
....
....
....

This made me **HAPPY:**

What the **FUCK?!**

....
....
....
....
....

My Mood Today (in pineapples)

Doodle **RANDOM FUCKERY** *here:*

Fuck yeah!

Celebrate something:

·····································
·····································
·····································
·····································
·····································

Fuck off.

Wave goodbye to negative thoughts:

·····································
·····································
·····································
·····································
·····································

SHIT *to remember:*

DATE:

___ / ___ / ___

DAY OF THE WEEK

S M T W T F S

ASHOLE of the DAY:

SORRY. *Not sorry.*

....

....

....

Something REDEEMING *about today:*

My Mood Today (in pineapples)

Today's **SHIT LIST**
(people, places, things):

☐ .... ☐ ....
☐ .... ☐ ....
☐ .... ☐ ....
☐ .... ☐ ....
☐ .... ☐

> Opinions *are like* **assholes.**
> **Everyone** *has one,*
> *and they are often* **full of shit.**

Fuck yeah!
I did this:

....
....
....
....
....

Unfuck yourself.
What makes you **SMILE** *most?*

....
....
....
....
....
....

DATE:

___ / ___ / ___

ASSHOLE *of the* DAY:

....
....
....
....
....

🍍 **FUCK YEAH!** 🍍

Grateful I did this today:

Happy I didn't do this today:

BITCH *session:*

....
....
....
....
....

I'm **LUCKY** *to have . . .*

....

....

....

JOURNAL SOME SHIT
that makes you laugh:

I've got an **ATTITUDE** *of* **GRATITUDE:**

....

....

....

Figure this the **FUCK** *out:*

1. FKUC TI: _____

2. HPENSHA PTIS: _____

3. SLNLT I UQEEA: _____

Answer: 1. FUCK IT 2. SHIT HAPPENS 3. STILL A QUEEN

My Mood Today (in pineapples)

🍍 🍍 🍍 🍍 🍍 🍍 🍍 🍍 🍍 🍍

DATE:

___ / ___ / ___

DAY OF THE WEEK

S M T W T F S

ASSHOLE *of the* **DAY:**

I'm **PROUD** *of myself for . . .*

SHIT *that makes me* **SMILE:**

My Mood Today (in pineapples)

**UNFUCK YOUR MIND.
WRITE YOUR AFFIRMATIONS.**

I am _____

I will _____

I love _____

What the fuck?!

I **LEARNED** *this today:*

....
....
....
....
....

BITCH *session:*

DATE:

___ / ___ / ___

DAY OF THE WEEK

S M T W T F S

ASSHOLE *of the* DAY:

....
....
....
....
....

🍍 **FUCK YEAH!** 🍍

Grateful I did this today:

Happy I didn't do this today:

REFLECT
My favorite bad-ass bitch:

....
....
....
....

Doodle some **SHIT** *here:*

A fucking masterpiece.

I'm letting this go:

....

....

....

I'm **LUCKY** *to have . . .*

My Mood Today (in pineapples)

DATE:

__ / __ / __

DAY OF THE WEEK

S M T W T F S

ASSHOLE *of the* DAY:

Maybe I shouldn't have done this:

....

....

....

....

....

I'm SMILING *because . . .*

My Mood Today (in pineapples)

CURRENT MOOD:

☐ Happy
☐ Inspired
☐ Bring me coffee. Now.
☐ Feisty
☐ Peaceful
☐ Other: _____

True happiness *can be found in* coffee *and* tacos. *But not together. That will give you the shits.*

Fuck yeah!

CELEBRATE *something:*

_____
_____
_____
_____
_____
_____
_____
_____
_____
_____

I'VE GOT FUCKING GOALS!
List three:

1. _____
2. _____
3. _____

DATE:

__ / __ / __

S M T W T F S

ASSHOLE *of the* DAY:

....
....
....
....
....

DAMN, *this felt good:*

🍍 | OH FUCK! | 🍍

This didn't go as planned: *I'll do this differently next time:*

....
....
....
....

Today's **SHIT LIST**
(people, places, things):

- [ ] ....
- [ ] ....
- [ ] ....
- [ ] ....
- [ ] ....

- [ ] ....
- [ ] ....
- [ ] ....
- [ ] ....
- [ ] ....

RANDOM SHIT
to accomplish this week:

BITCH session:

....

....

....

....

....

My Mood Today (in pineapples)

🍍 🍍 🍍 🍍 🍍 🍍 🍍 🍍 🍍 🍍

DATE:

__ / __ / __

DAY OF THE WEEK

S M T W T F S

ASSHOLE *of the* DAY:

 FUCK YEAH!

I'm grateful I did this today:

I'm happy I didn't do this today:

I'm LUCKY *to have* . . .

My Mood Today (in pineapples)

_____ YEAH!

CLUSTER _____

FAN _____ INGTASTIC

RANDOM SHIT
that makes me laugh:

Let some **SHIT** _go:_

DATE:

___ / ___ / ___

DAY OF THE WEEK

S **M** **T** **W** **T** **F** **S**

ASSHOLE *of the* DAY:

FUCK YEAH!

Grateful I did this today:

Happy I didn't do this today:

Oh, for fuck's sake.
This didn't go my way:

CURRENT MOOD:

- ☐ Happy
- ☐ Leave me the fuck alone.
- ☐ Snarling
- ☐ Sensitive
- ☐ So. Fucking. Tired.
- ☐ Other: _____

What the fuck?!

Tomorrow I'll do this **DIFFERENTLY:**

....

....

....

....

....

I've got an **ATTITUDE** *of* **GRATITUDE:**

My Mood Today (in pineapples)

DATE:

___ / ___ / ___

DAY OF THE WEEK

S M T W T F S

ASSHOLE *of the* DAY:

BITCH *session:*

COLOR THIS SHIT

TAKE NO SHIT. GIVE NO FUCKS.

Not giving a **FUCK**
is so much better than
REVENGE.

I'm lucky to have ...

....

....

....

....

....

....

What the **FUCK** *was this?!*

....

....

....

....

....

....

....

JOURNAL SOME SHIT
that you love about your home:

My Mood Today (in pineapples)

DATE:

___ / ___ / ___

DAY OF THE WEEK

(S) **S** (M) **T** (W) **T** (F) **S**

ASSHOLE *of the* DAY:

....
....
....
....
....

This made me **HAPPY:**

What the **FUCK** *was this?!*

....
....
....
....
....

My Mood Today (in pineapples)

Doodle **RANDOM FUCKERY** *here:*

SHIT *to remember:*

....
....
....
....

FUCK YEAH!
Celebrate something:

FUCK OFF.
Wave goodbye to negative thoughts:

DATE:

__ / __ / __

DAY OF THE WEEK

S M T W T F S

ASSHOLE *of the* DAY:

SORRY. *Not sorry.*

Something REDEEMING *about today:*

My Mood Today (in pineapples)

Today's SHIT LIST
(people, places, things):

- [ ] ....
- [ ] ....
- [ ] ....
- [ ] ....
- [ ] ....

- [ ] ....
- [ ] ....
- [ ] ....
- [ ] ....
- [ ] ....

FUCK YEAH!

I did this:

Unfuck yourself.

WHAT'S THE BIGGEST CHALLENGE
you've had to overcome?

....
....
....
....
....
....
....

DATE:

__ / __ / __

DAY OF THE WEEK

S M T W T F S

ASSHOLE *of the* DAY:

 FUCK YEAH!

I'm grateful I did this today:

I'm happy I didn't do this today:

BITCH *session:*

My Mood Today (in pineapples)

I'm a badass.

These things make me **SPECIAL:**

....

....

....

....

....

I've got an **ATTITUDE** *of* **GRATITUDE:**

Figure this the **FUCK** *out:*

VE'I TGO A DGOO RHETA,
UTB SHIT HMOUT!

_____

_____

DATE:

___ / ___ / ___

DAY OF THE WEEK

S **M** **T** **W** **T** **F** **S**

ASSHOLE *of the* **DAY:**

Fuck yeah!

I'm PROUD *of myself for:*

SHIT *that makes me* **SMILE:**

UNFUCK YOUR MIND.
WRITE YOUR AFFIRMATIONS.

I can _____

My body is _____

I choose _____

> ### THERAPY HELPS, BUT YELLING PROFANITY IS
>
> √ *Cheaper*
> √ *Faster*
> √ *More rewarding*

What the fuck?!

I **LEARNED** *this today:*

....
....
....
....
....

BITCH *session:*

My Mood Today (in pineapples)

DATE:

___ / ___ / ___

DAY OF THE WEEK

(S) (M) (T) (W) (T) (F) (S)

ASSHOLE *of the* DAY:

....

....

....

....

....

FUCK YEAH!

Grateful I did this today:

Happy I didn't do this today:

REFLECT
I'd shank a bitch for this meal:

....

....

....

....

....

Doodle some **SHIT** *here:*

FUCK IT!
I'm letting this go:

....

....

....

I'm **LUCKY** *to have . . .*

My Mood Today (in pineapples)

DATE:

___ / ___ / ___

DAY OF THE WEEK

S M T W T F S

ASSHOLE *of the* **DAY:**

Maybe I shouldn't have done this:

....

....

....

....

I'm **SMILING** *because* . . .

My Mood Today (in pineapples)

CURRENT MOOD:

- ☐ Happy
- ☐ Inspired
- ☐ Bring me coffee. Now.
- ☐ Feisty
- ☐ Peaceful
- ☐ Other: _____

FUCK YEAH!

CELEBRATE *something:*

I'VE GOT FUCKING GOALS.
List three to **ACCOMPLISH** *this week:*

1. _____
2. _____
3. _____

Let some **SHIT** *go:*

DATE:

___ / ___ / ___

DAY OF THE WEEK

S M T W T F S

ASSHOLE *of the* DAY:

....
....
....
....
....

DAMN, *this felt good:*

OH FUCK!

This didn't go as planned:

I'll do this differently next time:

....
....
....
....

RANDOM SHIT *I take for granted:*

BITCH *session:*

_____

_____

_____

_____

_____

_____

_____

_____

_____

_____

My Mood Today (in pineapples)

🍍 🍍 🍍 🍍 🍍 🍍 🍍 🍍 🍍 🍍

DATE:

___ / ___ / ___

DAY OF THE WEEK

S M T W T F S

ASSHOLE *of the* DAY:

🍍 FUCK YEAH! 🍍

Grateful I did this today:

Happy I didn't do this today:

I'm LUCKY *to have* . . .

FILL IN THE FUCKS:

Some days I feel stuck
between "_____ it"
and "what the _____?"

It may be a
shitshow.
But it's
My **shitshow.**

Let some **SHIT** *go:*

My Mood Today *(in pineapples)*

DATE:

DAY OF THE WEEK

__ / __ / __

(S) (M) (T) (W) (T) (F) (S)

ASSHOLE *of the* DAY:

....
....
....
....
....

FUCK YEAH!

Grateful I did this today:

Happy I didn't do this today:

FUCK *this* SHIT:

....
....
....
....
....

I'm over it.

CURRENT MOOD:

- [ ] Happy
- [ ] Leave me the fuck alone.
- [ ] Apathetic
- [ ] Thankful
- [ ] I'm just a tired-ass woman trying to survive.
- [ ] Other: _____

I've got an **ATTITUDE** *of* **GRATITUDE:**

What the **FUCK** *was I thinking?!*

My Mood Today (in pineapples)

DATE:

___ / ___ / ___

DAY OF THE WEEK

S M T W T F S

ASSHOLE *of the* DAY:

BITCH *session:*

COLOR THIS SHIT

I'M FUCKING AWESOME

> Little girls **CRY.**
> Big girls say
> **"FUCK."**

I'm lucky to have . . .

_____

_____

_____

_____

_____

_____

What the **FUCK** was this?!

_____

_____

_____

_____

_____

_____

_____

_____

_____

_____

_____

JOURNAL SOME SHIT
that makes you proud:

My Mood Today (in pineapples)

DATE:

___ / ___ / ___

DAY OF THE WEEK

(S) (M) (T) (W) (T) (F) (S)

ASSHOLE *of the* DAY:

This made me **HAPPY:**

What the **FUCK?!**

My Mood Today (in pineapples)

Doodle **RANDOM FUCKERY** *here:*

SHIT *to remember:*

_____

_____

_____

_____

_____

FUCK YEAH!

Celebrate something:

FUCK OFF.

Wave goodbye to negative thoughts:

DATE:

__ / __ / __

DAY OF THE WEEK

S M T W T F S

ASSHOLE *of the* DAY:

SORRY. *Not sorry.*

....

....

....

....

....

Something REDEEMING *about today:*

My Mood Today (in pineapples)

Today's **SHIT LIST**
(people, places, things):

☐ .... ☐ ....
☐ .... ☐ ....
☐ .... ☐ ....
☐ .... ☐ ....
☐   ☐

FUCK YEAH!

I did this:

....
....
....
....
....
....

> *I've stopped aiming for*
> **PERFECTION.**
> *I'm shooting for*
> **SURVIVAL.**

Unfuck yourself.

What is your **FAVORITE MEMORY** *of a relative?*

....
....
....
....
....
....
....
....
....
....
....

DATE:

__ / __ / __

DAY OF THE WEEK

S M T W T F S

ASSHOLE *of the* DAY:

....

....

....

....

....

FUCK YEAH!

Grateful I did this today:

Happy I didn't do this today:

BITCH *session:*

....

....

....

....

....

I've got an **ATTITUDE** _of_ **GRATITUDE:**

....

....

....

....

....

....

....

....

....

....

JOURNAL SOME SHIT
that you do when you're **STRESSED:**

Figure this the **FUCK** _out:_

**REAF FO ARELIFU SI
YM IGCFUNK UFEL.**

Answer: FEAR OF FAILURE IS MY FUCKING FUEL.

My Mood Today (in pineapples)

DATE:

___ / ___ / ___

DAY OF THE WEEK

S M T W T F S

ASSHOLE *of the* DAY:

I'm PROUD *of myself for:*

SHIT *that makes me* SMILE:

My Mood Today (in pineapples)

UNFUCK YOUR MIND.
WRITE YOUR AFFIRMATIONS.

I will _____

I accept _____

I allow _____

What the fuck?!

I LEARNED *this today:*

_____

_____

_____

_____

_____

_____

_____

_____

_____

_____

BITCH *session:*

DATE:

___ / ___ / ___

DAY OF THE WEEK

S M T W T F S

ASSHOLE *of the* DAY:

....

....

....

....

FUCK YEAH!

Grateful I did this today:

Happy I didn't do this today:

REFLECT
Shit I'm looking forward to:

....

....

....

....

Doodle some **SHIT** *here:*

FUCK IT!

I'm letting this go:

....

....

....

....

....

I'm **LUCKY** *to have* . . .

My Mood Today (in pineapples)

DATE:

___ / ___ / ___

DAY OF THE WEEK

S M T W T F S

ASSHOLE *of the* DAY:

Maybe I shouldn't have done this:

....

....

....

....

....

I'm **SMILING** *because* . . .

My Mood Today (in pineapples)

CURRENT MOOD:

- [ ] Bitchy
- [ ] Grateful
- [ ] Nope
- [ ] Very bitchy
- [ ] Other: _____

> The secret to
> **happiness**
> is to stay away
> from **assholes.**

Fuck yeah!

CELEBRATE *something:*

_____
_____
_____
_____
_____
_____
_____
_____

BITCH *session:*

DATE:

__ / __ / __

DAY OF THE WEEK

(S) (M) (T) (W) (T) (F) (S)

ASSHOLE *of the* DAY:

DAMN, *this felt good:*

OH FUCK!

This didn't go as planned:

I'll do this differently next time:

Today's **SHIT LIST**
(people, places, things):

☐ ....   ☐ ....
☐ ....   ☐ ....
☐ ....   ☐ ....
☐ ....   ☐ ....
☐ ....   ☐ ....

RANDOM SHIT
I'm proud of myself for:

BITCH *session:*

....

....

....

....

....

....

....

....

My Mood Today (in pineapples)

DATE:

___ / ___ / ___

DAY OF THE WEEK

S **M** **T** **W** **T** **F** **S**

ASSHOLE *of the* **DAY:**

 FUCK YEAH!

Grateful I did this today:

Happy I didn't do this today:

I'm LUCKY *to have . . .*

Write your own **FUCKING QUOTE:**

_____
_____
_____
_____
_____

RANDOM SHIT
I don't want to forget about:

Let some **SHIT** *go:*

_____
_____
_____
_____
_____
_____
_____
_____
_____
_____
_____

My Mood Today (in pineapples)

🍍 🍍 🍍 🍍 🍍 🍍 🍍 🍍 🍍 🍍

DATE:

___ / ___ / ___

DAY OF THE WEEK

(S) (M) (T) (W) (T) (F) (S)

ASSHOLE *of the* DAY:

FUCK YEAH!

Grateful I did this today:

Happy, I didn't do this today:

FUCK *this* SHIT:

CURRENT MOOD:

- ☐ Bitchy
- ☐ Fun
- ☐ Sensible
- ☐ Too tired for this shit
- ☐ Ew, people
- ☐ Other: _____

WHAT THE FUCK?!

Tomorrow I'll do this **DIFFERENTLY:**

I've got an **ATTITUDE** *of* **GRATITUDE:**

DATE:

__ / __ / __

DAY OF THE WEEK

(S) (M) (T) (W) (T) (F) (S)

ASSHOLE *of the* **DAY:**

BITCH *session:*

COLOR THIS SHIT

QUEEN OF THE SHITSHOW

LIFE LESSON 237,403:
You can't sprinkle **SUGAR** *on bullshit and call it a* **CUPCAKE.**

I'm **LUCKY** *to have . . .*

....
....
....
....

What the **FUCK** *was this?!*

....
....
....
....

JOURNAL SOME SHIT
What was your **HAPPIEST MOMENT** *last year?*

Why?

My Mood Today (in pineapples)

DATE:

__ / __ / __

S M T W T F S

ASSHOLE *of the* DAY:

....
....
....
....
....

This made me **HAPPY:**

What the **FUCK** *was this?!*

....
....
....
....
....

My Mood Today (in pineapples)

Doodle **RANDOM FUCKERY** *here:*

Fuck yeah!

CELEBRATE *something:*

FUCK OFF.

Wave goodbye to negative thoughts:

SHIT *to remember:*

DATE:

___ / ___ / ___

DAY OF THE WEEK

S M T W T F S

ASSHOLE *of the* DAY:

SORRY. *Not sorry.*

....

....

....

....

....

Find something **REDEEMING** *about today:*

My Mood Today (in pineapples)

Today's SHIT LIST
(people, places, things):

- ☐ ....
- ☐ ....
- ☐ ....
- ☐ ....
- ☐ ....

- ☐ ....
- ☐ ....
- ☐ ....
- ☐ ....
- ☐ ....

FUCK YEAH!

I did this:

Unfuck yourself.

I find **JOY** *in . . .*

....
....
....
....
....
....
....
....

Let some **SHIT** *go:*

DATE:

___ / ___ / ___

DAY OF THE WEEK

(S) (M) (T) (W) (T) (F) (S)

ASSHOLE *of the* DAY:

....
....
....
....
....

🍍 | FUCK YEAH! | 🍍

Grateful I did this today:

Happy I didn't do this today:

BITCH *session:*

....
....
....
....
....

I've got an **ATTITUDE** *of* **GRATITUDE:**

....

....

....

JOURNAL SOME SHIT
that you find inspiring:

Figure this the **FUCK** *out:*

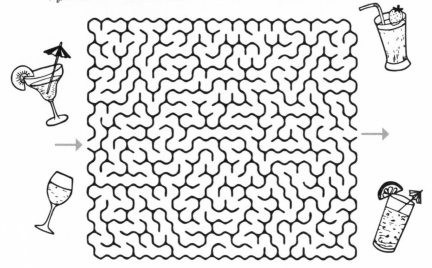

My Mood Today (in pineapples)

DATE:

DAY OF THE WEEK

___ / ___ / ___

S   M   T   W   T   F   S

ASSHOLE *of the* DAY:

I'm PROUD *of myself for* . . .

SHIT *that makes me* SMILE:

My Mood Today (in pineapples)

UNFUCK YOUR MIND.
WRITE YOUR AFFIRMATIONS.

I love _____

I control _____

I am _____

I'd rather be stuck on an island **alone** than stuck in a room with an **asshole.**

What the fuck?!

I **LEARNED** *this today:*

....
....
....
....
....

BITCH *session:*

DATE:

___ / ___ / ___

DAY OF THE WEEK

(S) (M) (T) (W) (T) (F) (S)

ASSHOLE *of the* DAY:

....
....
....
....
....

FUCK YEAH!

Grateful I did this today:

Happy I didn't do this today:

REFLECT
The best part of my day:

....
....
....
....
....
....

Doodle some **SHIT** *here:*

FUCK IT!
I'm letting this go:

....

....

....

....

....

I'm **LUCKY** *to have . . .*

My Mood Today (in pineapples)

DATE:

___ / ___ / ___

DAY OF THE WEEK

S M T W T F S

ASSHOLE *of the* DAY:

Maybe I shouldn't have done this:

I'm SMILING *because* . . .

My Mood Today (in pineapples)

CURRENT MOOD:

☐ Happy
☐ Inspired
☐ Bring me coffee. Now.
☐ Feisty
☐ Peaceful
☐ Other: _____

Fuck yeah!

CELEBRATE *something:*

_____
_____
_____
_____
_____
_____
_____

I'VE GOT FUCKING GOALS.

List at least one you've **ACCOMPLISHED** *this week:*

DATE:

___ / ___ / ___

DAY OF THE WEEK

S M T W T F S

ASSHOLE *of the* DAY:

DAMN, *this felt good:*

OH FUCK!

This didn't go as planned:

I'll do this differently next time:

Today's SHIT LIST
(*people, places, things*):

- [ ] ....
- [ ] ....
- [ ] ....
- [ ] ....
- [ ] ....

- [ ] ....
- [ ] ....
- [ ] ....
- [ ] ....
- [ ] ....

RANDOM SHIT
I love to do:

BITCH *session:*

....
....
....
....
....

My Mood Today (in pineapples)

🍍 🍍 🍍 🍍 🍍 🍍 🍍 🍍 🍍 🍍

DATE:

__ / __ / __

DAY OF THE WEEK

S M T W T F S

ASSHOLE *of the* DAY:

 FUCK YEAH!

Grateful I did this today:

....
....
....
....
....

Happy I didn't do this today:

....
....
....
....
....

I'm LUCKY *to have . . .*

FILL IN THE FUCKS:

Adulthood is an alternating series of "_____
this shit" and "what the _____" whispers
every time I leave my house.

I've got an ATTITUDE of GRATITUDE:

Let some SHIT go:

My Mood Today (in pineapples)

DATE:

__ / __ / __

ASSHOLE *of the* DAY:

....
....
....
....
....

🍍 | FUCK YEAH! | 🍍

Grateful I did this today:

Happy I didn't do this today:

Oh, for fuck's sake.

This didn't go MY WAY:

....
....
....
....
....
....

CURRENT MOOD:

☐ Nope
☐ Quirky
☐ Boss bitch
☐ Sensitive
☐ Still a tired-ass woman
☐ Other: _____

WHAT THE FUCK?!

Something I'll do **DIFFERENTLY** *tomorrow:*

I've got an **ATTITUDE** *of* **GRATITUDE:**

My Mood Today (in pineapples)

DATE:

___ / ___ / ___

DAY OF THE WEEK

S M T W T F S

ASSHOLE *of the* DAY:

BITCH *session:*

COLOR THIS SHIT

I WILL GET ALL THE SHIT DONE. LATER.

Today's **SHIT LIST**
(people, places, things):

☐ ....   ☐ ....
☐ ....   ☐ ....
☐ ....   ☐ ....
☐ ....   ☐ ....

I'm **LUCKY** *to have . . .*

What the **FUCK** *was this?!*

....

....

....

JOURNAL SOME SHIT
that makes you feel special:

My Mood Today (in pineapples)

🍍 🍍 🍍 🍍 🍍 🍍 🍍 🍍 🍍 🍍

DATE:

___ / ___ / ___

DAY OF THE WEEK

(S) (M) (T) (W) (T) (F) (S)

ASSHOLE *of the* DAY:

....
....
....
....
....

This made me **HAPPY:**

What the **FUCK?!**

....
....
....
....
....

My Mood Today (in pineapples)

Doodle **RANDOM FUCKERY** *here:*

Fuck yeah!

CELEBRATE *something:*

....

....

....

....

FUCK OFF.

Wave goodbye to negative thoughts:

SHIT *to remember:*

....

....

....

....

DATE:

__ / __ / __

DAY OF THE WEEK

S M T W T F S

ASSHOLE *of the* DAY:

SORRY. *Not sorry.*

Something **REDEEMING** *about today:*

My Mood Today (in pineapples)

Today's **SHIT LIST**
(people, places, things):

- [ ] ....
- [ ] ....
- [ ] ....
- [ ] ....
- [ ] ....

- [ ] ....
- [ ] ....
- [ ] ....
- [ ] ....
- [ ] ....

REMINDER:

The older you get,

the more everyone can

KISS YOUR ASS!

Fuck yeah!
I did this:

....

....

....

....

....

UNFUCK YOURSELF.

What do I keep **PROCRASTINATING** *about?*

How will I **FIX** *it?*

DATE:

___ / ___ / ___

DAY OF THE WEEK

S M T W T F S

ASSHOLE *of the* DAY:

....
....
....
....
....

🍍 | FUCK YEAH! | 🍍

Grateful I did this today:

Happy I didn't do this today:

BITCH *session:*

....
....
....
....
....

I'm **LUCKY** *to have* . . .

_____

_____

_____

_____

_____

JOURNAL SOME SHIT
that no one knows about:

I've got an **ATTITUDE** *of* **GRATITUDE:**

_____

_____

_____

_____

_____

_____

My Mood Today (in pineapples)

🍍 🍍 🍍 🍍 🍍 🍍 🍍 🍍 🍍 🍍

DATE:

___ / ___ / ___

DAY OF THE WEEK

(S) (M) (T) (W) (T) (F) (S)

ASSHOLE *of the* DAY:

I'm PROUD *of myself for:*

....

....

....

SHIT *that makes me* SMILE:

My Mood Today (in pineapples)

UNFUCK YOUR MIND.
WRITE YOUR AFFIRMATIONS.

I am _____

I will _____

I love _____

WHAT THE FUCK?!

I **LEARNED** *this today:*

BITCH *session:*

DATE:

__ / __ / __

DAY OF THE WEEK

S M T W T F S

ASSHOLE *of the* DAY:

....
....
....
....

🍍 FUCK YEAH! 🍍

Grateful I did this today:

Happy I didn't do this today:

REFLECT
My favorite badass bitch:

....
....
....
....

Doodle some **SHIT** *here:*

FUCK IT!
I'm letting this go:

....

....

....

....

I'm **LUCKY** *to have . . .*

My Mood Today (in pineapples)

DATE:

__ / __ / __

DAY OF THE WEEK

(S) (M) (T) (W) (T) (F) (S)

ASSHOLE *of the* DAY:

Maybe I shouldn't have done this:

....

....

....

....

....

I'm SMILING *because . . .*

My Mood Today (in pineapples)

CURRENT MOOD:

- [ ] Happy
- [ ] Inspired
- [ ] Bring me coffee. Now.
- [ ] Feisty
- [ ] Peaceful
- [ ] Other: _____

I'm just a sensitive **hot mess** *filled with* **f-bombs** *and* **sunshine.**

Fuck yeah!

CELEBRATE *something:*

I'VE GOT FUCKING GOALS.
List three:

1. _____
2. _____
3. _____

DATE:

__ / __ / __

DAY OF THE WEEK

S M T W T F S

ASSHOLE *of the* DAY:

....

....

....

....

....

DAMN, *this felt good:*

OH FUCK!

This didn't go as planned:

I'll do this differently next time:

Today's **SHIT LIST**
(people, places, things):

☐ ....   ☐ ....
☐ ....   ☐ ....
☐ ....   ☐ ....
☐ ....   ☐ ....
☐ ....   ☐ ....

RANDOM SHIT

Songs I love to **DANCE** *to:*

BITCH *session:*

....
....
....
....
....
....
....
....
....

My Mood Today (in pineapples)

🍍 🍍 🍍 🍍 🍍 🍍 🍍 🍍 🍍 🍍

DATE:

__ / __ / __

DAY OF THE WEEK

(S) (M) (T) (W) (T) (F) (S)

ASSHOLE *of the* **DAY:**

 FUCK YEAH!

I'm grateful I did this:

....
....
....
....

I'm happy I didn't do this today:

....
....
....
....

I'm **LUCKY** *to have* . . .

My Mood Today (in pineapples)

FILL IN THE FUCKS.

Don't let _____ ers steal your shine.

Tell them to _____ off instead.

Something I need to **UNFUCK:**

Let some **SHIT** *go:*

DATE:

___ / ___ / ___

DAY OF THE WEEK

S M T W T F S

ASSHOLE *of the* DAY:

....
....
....
....
....

🍍 | FUCK YEAH! | 🍍

Grateful I did this today:

Happy I didn't do this today:

Oh, for fuck's sake.
This didn't go **MY WAY:**

....
....
....
....
....
....

CURRENT MOOD:

- [ ] Happy
- [ ] Leave me the fuck alone.
- [ ] Snarling
- [ ] Sensitive
- [ ] So. Fucking. Tired.
- [ ] Other: _____

WHAT THE FUCK?!

Tomorrow I'll do this **DIFFERENTLY:**

I've got an **ATTITUDE** *of* **GRATITUDE:**

My Mood Today (in pineapples)

DATE:

___ / ___ / ___

DAY OF THE WEEK

S M T W T F S

ASSHOLE *of the* **DAY:**

BITCH *session:*

> *Before you judge me, know that* **I don't give a fuck.**

I'm lucky to have . . .

_____

_____

_____

_____

_____

_____

What the **FUCK** *was this?!*

_____

_____

_____

_____

_____

_____

_____

_____

JOURNAL SOME SHIT
that you can't live without:

My Mood Today (in pineapples)

DATE:

___ / ___ / ___

DAY OF THE WEEK

(S) (M) (T) (W) (T) (F) (S)

ASSHOLE *of the* DAY:

....
....
....
....
....

This made me **HAPPY:**

What the **FUCK** *was this?!*

....
....
....
....

My Mood Today (in pineapples)

Doodle **RANDOM FUCKERY** *here:*

Fuck yeah!

Celebrate something:

....

....

....

....

....

Fuck off.

Wave goodbye to negative thoughts:

....

....

....

....

....

SHIT *to remember:*

DATE:

__ / __ / __

DAY OF THE WEEK

S M T W T F S

ASSHOLE *of the* **DAY:**

SORRY. *Not sorry.*

Something **REDEEMING** *about today:*

My Mood Today (in pineapples)

Today's **SHIT LIST**
(people, places, things):

- [ ] ....
- [ ] ....
- [ ] ....
- [ ] ....
- [ ] ....

- [ ] ....
- [ ] ....
- [ ] ....
- [ ] ....
- [ ] ....

FUCK YEAH!

I did this:

Unfuck yourself...
What do *I* want to **DO MORE** of?

....

....

....

....

....

....

....

....

DATE:

___ / ___ / ___

DAY OF THE WEEK

S M T W T F S

ASSHOLE *of the* DAY:

....
....
....
....
....

🍍 **FUCK YEAH!** 🍍

Grateful I did this today:

Happy I didn't do this today:

BITCH *session:*

....
....
....
....
....
....

I'M A BADASS.
I love this about MY BODY:

I've got an ATTITUDE *of* GRATITUDE:

Figure this the FUCK *out:*

OREVYEEN ASW ININTKHG TI.
I JTUS DAIS TI.

My Mood Today (in pineapples)

DATE:

___ / ___ / ___

DAY OF THE WEEK

S **M** **T** **W** **T** **F** **S**

ASSHOLE *of the* **DAY:**

FUCK YEAH!
I'm **PROUD** *of myself for:*

SHIT *that makes me smile:*

My Mood Today (in pineapples)

UNFUCK YOUR MIND.
WRITE YOUR AFFIRMATIONS.

I can _____

My body is _____

I choose _____

Today's mood:

FUCK IT.

I should've stayed in bed.

What the fuck?!

I **LEARNED** *this today:*

....
....
....
....
....

BITCH *session:*

DATE:

___ / ___ / ___

DAY OF THE WEEK

(S) (M) (T) (W) (T) (F) (S)

ASSHOLE *of the* DAY:

....

....

....

....

....

FUCK YEAH!

Grateful I did this today:

Happy I didn't do this today:

REFLECT

What's an "Oh shit" moment you recently had?

....

....

....

....

Doodle some **SHIT** *here:*

FUCK IT!
I'm letting this go:

....

....

....

....

I'm **LUCKY** *to have . . .*

My Mood Today (in pineapples)

DATE:

___ / ___ / ___

DAY OF THE WEEK

S M T W T F S

ASSHOLE *of the* DAY:

Maybe I shouldn't have done this:

....
....
....
....
....

I'm SMILING *because* . . .

My Mood Today (in pineapples)

CURRENT MOOD:

- ☐ Happy
- ☐ Inspired
- ☐ Bring me coffee. Now.
- ☐ Feisty
- ☐ Peaceful
- ☐ Other: _____

Fuck yeah!

CELEBRATE *something:*

_____

_____

_____

_____

_____

I'VE GOT FUCKING GOALS.

List three to **ACCOMPLISH** *this year:*

1. _____
2. _____
3. _____

Let some **SHIT** *go:*

_____

_____

_____

_____

_____

DATE:

___ / ___ / ___

DAY OF THE WEEK

(S) (M) (T) (W) (T) (F) (S)

ASSHOLE *of the* DAY:

....
....
....
....
....

DAMN, *this felt good:*

🍍 OH FUCK! 🍍

This didn't go as planned: *I'll do this differently next time:*

RANDOM SHIT
I need to organize:

I'M A BADASS.
I do this **BETTER** *than anyone I know:*

BITCH *session:*

My Mood Today (in pineapples)

DATE:

__ / __ / __

DAY OF THE WEEK

S M T W T F S

ASSHOLE *of the* DAY:

🍍 FUCK YEAH! 🍍

Grateful I did this today:

Happy, I didn't do this today:

I'm LUCKY *to have* . . .

FILL IN THE FUCKS:

Row, row, row your boat gently the
_____ away from me.

The **bitch** in me wants to **laugh** at you. She wins.

Let some **SHIT** *go:*

My Mood Today (in pineapples)

DATE:

__ / __ / __

DAY OF THE WEEK

S M T W T F S

ASSHOLE *of the* DAY:

....
....
....
....
....

FUCK YEAH!

Grateful I did this today:

Happy I didn't do this today:

FUCK *this* SHIT:

....
....
....
....
....
....

CURRENT MOOD:

☐ Happy

☐ Leave me the fuck alone.

☐ Apathetic

☐ Thankful

☐ I'm just a tired-ass woman trying to survive.

☐ Other: _____

I've got an ATTITUDE *of* GRATITUDE:

....

....

....

....

....

WHAT THE FUCK?!

I LEARNED *this today:*

My Mood Today (in pineapples)

DATE:

___ / ___ / ___

DAY OF THE WEEK

S M T W T F S

ASSHOLE *of the* DAY:

BITCH *session:*

I'm **LUCKY** to have . . .

_____

_____

_____

_____

_____

What the **FUCK** was I thinking?!

JOURNAL SOME SHIT
that helps you **RELAX:**

_____

_____

_____

_____

_____

_____

_____

_____

My Mood Today (in pineapples)

DATE:

___ / ___ / ___

DAY OF THE WEEK

(S) (M) (T) (W) (T) (F) (S)

ASSHOLE *of the* DAY:

....
....
....
....
....

This made me **HAPPY:**

What the **FUCK?!**

....
....
....
....
....

My Mood Today (in pineapples)

🍍 🍍 🍍 🍍 🍍 🍍 🍍 🍍 🍍 🍍

Doodle **RANDOM FUCKERY** *here:*

Fuck yeah!

CELEBRATE *something:*

FUCK OFF.

Wave goodbye to negative thoughts:

SHIT *to remember:*

DATE:

__ / __ / __

DAY OF THE WEEK

S M T W T F S

ASSHOLE *of the* DAY:

SORRY. *Not sorry.*

Something **REDEEMING** *about today:*

My Mood Today (in pineapples)

Today's **SHIT LIST**
(people, places, things):

- [ ] ....
- [ ] ....
- [ ] ....
- [ ] ....
- [ ] ....

- [ ] ....
- [ ] ....
- [ ] ....
- [ ] ....
- [ ] ....

> *Why the* **fuck** *are you trying to fit in someone's* **box?** *Tell them to shove their* **box** *up their* **ass.**

Unfuck yourself.

Write a letter to your **FUTURE SELF:**

....
....
....
....
....
....
....
....
....
....
....
....
....

DATE:

DAY OF THE WEEK

__ / __ / __

S M T W T F S

ASSHOLE *of the* DAY:

....

....

....

....

....

FUCK YEAH!

Grateful I did this today:

Happy, I didn't do this today:

BITCH *session:*

....

....

....

....

....

....

I've got an **ATTITUDE** *of* **GRATITUDE:**

....

....

....

....

....

JOURNAL SOME SHIT
that is **BEAUTIFUL:**

Figure this the **FUCK** *out:*

A TELILT BTI FO CYRKUFE NAC KEMA A DYA A TOL MOER FNU!

A _____ A _____ A _____

Answer: A LITTLE BIT OF FUCKERY CAN MAKE A DAY A LOT MORE FUN!

My Mood Today (in pineapples)

🍍 🍍 🍍 🍍 🍍 🍍 🍍 🍍 🍍 🍍

DATE:

___ / ___ / ___

DAY OF THE WEEK

S M T W T F S

ASHOLE *of the* DAY:

I'm PROUD *of myself for* . . .

SHIT *that makes me* SMILE:

My Mood Today (in pineapples)

UNFUCK YOUR MIND.
WRITE YOUR AFFIRMATIONS.

I will _____

I accept _____

I allow _____

WHAT THE FUCK?!

I **LEARNED** *this today:*

BITCH *session:*

DATE:

___ / ___ / ___

DAY OF THE WEEK

(S) (M) (T) (W) (T) (F) (S)

ASSHOLE *of the* DAY:

....
....
....
....
....

🍍 | FUCK YEAH! | 🍍

Grateful I did this today:

Happy I didn't do this today:

REFLECT
A badass boy I love:

....
....
....
....
....
....

Doodle some **SHIT** *here:*

FUCK IT!

I'm letting this go:

....

....

....

....

....

I'm **LUCKY** *to have . . .*

My Mood Today (in pineapples)

DATE:

__ / __ / __

DAY OF THE WEEK

S M T W T F S

ASSHOLE *of the* **DAY:**

Maybe I shouldn't have done this:

....
....
....
....

I'm **SMILING** *because . . .*

My Mood Today (in pineapples)

CURRENT MOOD:

- ☐ Happy
- ☐ Bitchy
- ☐ Grateful
- ☐ Appreciative
- ☐ Nope
- ☐ Other: _____

Tomorrow [tuh-mo-row] noun.

A mythical land where I get all my shit done.

Fuck yeah!

CELEBRATE *something:*

_____

_____

_____

_____

_____

BITCH *session:*

DATE:

___ / ___ / ___

DAY OF THE WEEK

(S) (M) (T) (W) (T) (F) (S)

ASSHOLE *of the* DAY:

....
....
....
....
....

DAMN, *this felt good:*

OH FUCK!

This didn't go as planned:

....
....
....
....
....

I'll do this differently next time:

....
....
....
....
....

Today's **SHIT LIST**
(people, places, things):

- [ ] ....
- [ ] ....
- [ ] ....
- [ ] ....
- [ ] ....

- [ ] ....
- [ ] ....
- [ ] ....
- [ ] ....
- [ ] ....

RANDOM SHIT

Skills I'm **THANKFUL** I have:

BITCH session:

....
....
....
....
....
....
....
....

My Mood Today (in pineapples)

🍍 🍍 🍍 🍍 🍍 🍍 🍍 🍍 🍍 🍍

DATE:

___ / ___ / ___

DAY OF THE WEEK

S M T W T F S

ASSHOLE *of the* **DAY:**

 | FUCK YEAH! |

Grateful I did this today:

....
....
....
....

Happy I didn't do this today:

....
....
....
....

I'm **LUCKY** *to have . . .*

My Mood Today (in pineapples)

Write your own **FUCKING QUOTE:**

....

....

....

....

....

UNFUCK IT.

What's the **BIGGEST OBSTACLE** *you have right now?*

How will you **FIX** *it?*

Let some **SHIT** *go:*

....

....

....

....

....

....

....

....

DATE:

___ / ___ / ___

DAY OF THE WEEK

(S) (M) (T) (W) (T) (F) (S)

ASSHOLE *of the* DAY:

....

....

....

....

....

FUCK YEAH!

Grateful I did this today:

Happy I didn't do this today:

FUCK *this* SHIT:

....

....

....

....

....

....

....

- ☐ Bitchy
- ☐ Fun
- ☐ Sensible
- ☐ Too tired for this shit
- ☐ Ew, people
- ☐ Other: _____

WHAT THE FUCK?!

Tomorrow I'll do this **DIFFERENTLY:**

I've got an **ATTITUDE** *of* **GRATITUDE:**

DATE:

___ / ___ / ___

DAY OF THE WEEK

(S) (M) (T) (W) (T) (F) (S)

ASSHOLE *of the* DAY:

BITCH *session:*

COLOR THIS SHIT

MY MIDDLE FINGER SALUTES YOU.

Today's blessing: May your **coffee** *be warm and your* **shit list** *be small.*

I'm **LUCKY** *to have . . .*

What the **FUCK** was this?!

JOURNAL SOME SHIT
When do you feel **TRUE HAPPINESS?**

My Mood Today (in pineapples)

DATE:

__ / __ / __

DAY OF THE WEEK

(S) (M) (T) (W) (T) (F) (S)

ASSHOLE *of the* DAY:

....
....
....
....
....

This made me **HAPPY:**

What the **FUCK** *was this?!*

....
....
....
....
....

My Mood Today (in pineapples)

Doodle **RANDOM FUCKERY** *here:*

Fuck yeah!
CELEBRATE *something:*

FUCK OFF.

Wave goodbye to negative thoughts:

SHIT *to remember:*

DATE:

___ / ___ / ___

DAY OF THE WEEK

(S) (M) (T) (W) (T) (F) (S)

ASSHOLE *of the* **DAY:**

SORRY. *Not sorry.*

Find something **REDEEMING** *about today:*

My Mood Today (in pineapples)

Today's **SHIT LIST**
(people, places, things):

☐ ....   ☐ ....
☐ ....   ☐ ....
☐ ....   ☐ ....
☐ ....   ☐ ....
☐ ....   ☐ ....

FUCK YEAH!

I did this:

Unfuck yourself.
When do you feel most at **PEACE?**

....
....
....
....
....

Let some **SHIT** *go:*

DATE:

___ / ___ / ___

DAY OF THE WEEK

S **M** **T** **W** **T** **F** **S**

ASSHOLE *of the* DAY:

....
....
....
....
....

FUCK YEAH!

Grateful I did this today:

Happy, I didn't do this today:

BITCH *session:*

....
....
....
....
....
....
....
....

I've got an **ATTITUDE** *of* **GRATITUDE:**

....

....

....

....

....

....

....

....

....

....

JOURNAL SOME SHIT
that gives you **HAPPY TINGLES:**

Figure this the **FUCK** *out:*

ERSCU A LTETLI ADN RYRCA
HTE FCKU NO.

_____ A _____

Answer: CURSE A LITTLE AND CARRY THE FUCK ON.

My Mood Today (in pineapples)

DATE:

__ / __ / __

DAY OF THE WEEK

S **M** **T** **W** **T** **F** **S**

ASSHOLE *of the* **DAY:**

I'm **PROUD** *of myself for:*

SHIT *that makes me* **SMILE:**

My Mood Today (in pineapples)

UNFUCK YOUR MIND.
WRITE YOUR AFFIRMATIONS.

I love _____

I control _____

I am _____

Don't trust anyone who can't drop a good **F-BOMB.**

What the fuck?!

I **LEARNED** *this today:*

BITCH *session:*

DATE:

___ / ___ / ___

DAY OF THE WEEK

(S) (M) (T) (W) (T) (F) (S)

ASSHOLE *of the* DAY:

....
....
....
....

🍍 FUCK YEAH! 🍍

Grateful I did this today:

Happy I didn't do this today:

REFLECT
The best part of my day:

....
....
....
....

Doodle some **SHIT** *here:*

FUCK IT!
I'm letting this go:

I'm **LUCKY** *to have . . .*

My Mood Today (in pineapples)

DATE:

DAY OF THE WEEK

___ / ___ / ___

S **M** **T** **W** **T** **F** **S**

ASSHOLE *of the* **DAY:**

Maybe I shouldn't have done this:

....
....
....

I'm **SMILING** *because* . . .

My Mood Today (in pineapples)

CURRENT MOOD:

- ☐ Happy
- ☐ Inspired
- ☐ Bring me coffee. Now.
- ☐ Feisty
- ☐ Peaceful
- ☐ Other: _____

Don't let **FUCKERS** *dull your* **SPARKLE.**

Fuck yeah!

Give yourself a **COMPLIMENT:**

I'VE GOT FUCKING GOALS.

List at least one you've **ACCOMPLISHED** *this week:*

DATE:

___ / ___ / ___

DAY OF THE WEEK

S M T W T F S

ASSHOLE *of the* DAY:

....
....
....
....
....

DAMN, *this felt good:*

OH FUCK!

This didn't go as planned:

....
....
....
....

I'll do this differently next time:

....
....
....
....

Today's SHIT LIST
(people, places, things):

- ☐ ....
- ☐ ....
- ☐ ....
- ☐ ....
- ☐ ....

- ☐ ....
- ☐ ....
- ☐ ....
- ☐ ....

RANDOM SHIT
I want to REMEMBER:

BITCH *session:*

....
....
....
....
....
....
....

My Mood Today (in pineapples)

🍍 🍍 🍍 🍍 🍍 🍍 🍍 🍍 🍍 🍍

DATE:

__ / __ / __

DAY OF THE WEEK

S M T W T F S

ASSHOLE *of the* DAY:

 FUCK YEAH!

Grateful I did this today:

Happy, I didn't do this today:

I'm LUCKY *to have . . .*

FILL IN THE FUCKS.

Feeling fresh out of _____ today.

You used the last _____ I had to give.

I've got an **ATTITUDE** *of* **GRATITUDE:**

Let some **SHIT** *go:*

My Mood Today (in pineapples)

ABOUT THE AUTHOR

Kristie Breen is the author of the Fuck This Shitshow series of journals and planners. After juggling the bullshit that comes with being an avid hockey mom to three active boys and holding down a nine to five, Kristie would often find comfort in venting to her besties with some profanity-laced rants and a cocktail. Having spent her earlier days in publishing, Kristie harnessed her alter ego and launched her first bestselling journal, *Fuck This Shitshow: A Gratitude Journal for Tired-Ass Women* under the Crazy Tired Beetches brand. A first of its kind, *Fuck This Shitshow* has sold over 150,000 copies and continues to top Amazon bestseller lists. Today, Kristie is a mompreneur who spends the majority of her free time freezing her ass off in hockey rinks across the Northeast, cheering on her boys from the stands, and even enjoying the occasional date night with her husband of twenty years.